D. W. (David W.) Wood

History of the 20th O.V.V.I. Regiment

and proceedings of the first reunion at Mt. Vernon, Ohio, April 6, 1876

D. W. (David W.) Wood

History of the 20th O.V.V.I. Regiment
and proceedings of the first reunion at Mt. Vernon, Ohio, April 6, 1876

ISBN/EAN: 9783741170379

Manufactured in Europe, USA, Canada, Australia, Japa

Cover: Foto ©Thomas Meinert / pixelio.de

Manufactured and distributed by brebook publishing software
(www.brebook.com)

D. W. (David W.) Wood

History of the 20th O.V.V.I. Regiment

HISTORY

—OF THE—

20th 𝔒. 𝔙. 𝔙. 𝕴. Regiment,

—AND—

PROCEEDINGS OF THE FIRST REUNION

At Mt. Vernon, Ohio,

April 6, 1876.

COMPILED AND ARRANGED FOR PUBLICATION BY D. W. WOOD, MT. VERNON, OHIO.

COLUMBUS
PAUL & THRALL, BOOK AND JOB PRINTERS
1876.

Silver Cornet Band at the head, took up their line
of march to the depot of the C., Mt. V. & C. Railroad, to meet Generals M. F. Force, of Cincinnati,
and M. D. Leggett, of Cleveland. After their arrival the line was again formed under command of
Capt. D. W. Wood, and they were escorted through
the streets to Kirk Hall, where the exercises of the
day took place.

The hall was tastefully and appropriately decorated with flags, emblems, mottoes and evergreen.
The stage, on one side, contained a stack of arms,
the other a tasty memorial monument, while at the
rear had been erected a camp tent beautifully ornamented with evergreens. On the walls at the
north and south sides of the hall in gilt letters,
were the names of the battles in which the regiment participated, as follows: Fayetteville, Goldsboro, Ackworth, Atlanta, Bolivar, Raleigh, Kennesaw, Jackson, Raymond, Cheraw, Iuka, Champion Hill, Chattanooga, Orangeburg, Jonesboro,
Savannah, Columbia, Port Gibson, Last Point,
Grand Gulf, Vicksburg, Marietta, Shiloh.

At 2 o'clock P. M., the meeting was called to
order by Capt. D. W. Wood, Chairman of the
Committee of Arrangements.

Col. C. Garis, of Washington, O., W. A. Nut,
of Quincy, O., and J. A. Tilton, of Mt. Vernon,
were chosen Secretaries.

Hon. R. C. Kirk was introduced to the meeting,
and in a few well chosen remarks welcomed the
members of the regiment to the hospitalities of
the city.

Gen. Manning F. Force, of Cincinnati, was then
introduced, and delivered the annual address, giv-

ing a chronological history of the regiment, from the time of its organization at Camp Chase, in 1861, until it was disbanded in Columbus, in 1865.

Col. Chas. Whittlesey, of Cleveland, the "Father of the Regiment," then came to the front, and gave a more detailed account of the organization of the regiment, and its movements up to the time of his resignation, after the battle of Shiloh.

At the conclusion of his remarks, Wm. J. McFeeley, of Mt. Vernon, volunteered and sang the "Union Forever."

Maj. Gen. M. D. Leggett, was then introduced, and entertained the audience in a speech of considerable length, in which he gave the 20th Regiment great credit for the part it took during the war, and which, as their division commander, he was enabled to do with justice and precision.

Col. Harry Wilson, the first junior Lieutenant at the organization of the regiment, and its last Colonel, was then introduced, and made a few happy remarks, calling vividly to mind the many eccentricities of different individuals. His speech was well received.

At the conclusion of the speeches, the audience rose and joined in the chorus, " Rally 'Round the Flag."

A business meeting then took place, and the following officers were elected for the ensuing year:

President—Gen. Manning T. Force.

Secretary—Col. Harry Wilson.

A committee of five was appointed to have the proceedings of the meeting published in pamphlet form, and also to procure the names of all members of the regiment who have died since its organization, and draft suitable resolutions to their memory, reporting at the next annual meeting. The following gentlemen were appointed said committee: J. C. Gordon, B. A. F. Greer, D. W. Wood, J. A. Tilton, and J. G. Stevenson.

It was decided to hold the next reunion at Sidney, Ohio, July 22, 1877.

The President and Secretary were instructed to appoint a suitable person to deliver the next annual address.

Adjourned to supper.

The banquet was held at Banning Hall, which was beautifully trimmed for the occasion with flags and flowers. After doing ample justice to the delicacies prepared by the ladies, the following toasts were read and responded to in their order:

1. "The Enlisted Men."—Gen. M. F. Force.
2. "The Army of the Tennessee."—Gen. M. D. Leggett.
3. "One Union and One Flag."—Hon. R. C. Kirk.
4. "The Army and Navy."—Gen. Geo. W. Morgan.
5. "The Generals of the Army."—Rev. J. H. Hamilton.
6. "Gen. J. B. McPherson."—Col. Chas. Whittlesey.
7. "The Tree of Liberty," accompanied by a letter, proposed by Mrs. R. Raymond, aged 78 years—Response by Col. Harry Wilson.
8. "Our Ladies."—Capt. L. Y. Mitchell.
9. "The Bummers."—Private Leroy G. Hunt.
10. "The Officers of the 20th Ohio Regiment, and the Seventeenth Army Corps."—Capt. D. W. Wood.
11. "The Widows and Orphans."

It was intended that the response to this toast should be given by Chaplain Geo. W. Pepper, but that gentleman not being present, the response was omitted.

The following resolution was unanimously adopted at the conclusion of the exercises:

Resolved, That the most hearty thanks of the Veterans of the Old 20th O. V. V. I. are due and are hereby tendered to the citizens of Mt. Vernon, and the Committee of Arrangements, for the magnificent reception given to us this day.

The day's festivities closed by a grand social Hop at Kirk Hall in the evening, which was largely attended by the "beauty and the chivalry." The music was good, and unalloyed pleasure reigned throughout the evening.

20th Ohio Regiment.

Field and Staff—Non-Veteran.

CHARLES WHITTLESEY, Colonel from August 19, 1861, to April 19, 1862.

M. F. FORCE, Colonel, April 19, 1862, Brigadier General, April 11, 1863.

JOHN R. BOND, Adjutant, promoted to Major 67th O. V. I., October 1, 1861.

E. N. OWENS, Adjutant, promoted to Major 9th La. Vol., African Descent.

P. M. HITCHCOCK, Reg't Quartermaster, mustered out August 20, 1864.

E. L. HILL, Surgeon, mustered out October 11, 1864.

JAMES R. KNAPP, Chaplain, resigned April 19, 1862.

J. W. ALDERMAN,   "   "   March 22, 1863.

J. G. PURPLE, Assistant Surgeon, died at Nashville, Tennessee, May 26, 1862.

A. H. HUMISTON, Sergeant Major, promoted to Lieutenant Co. D., March 31, 1862.

J. B. WALKER, Sergeant Major, promoted to Lieutenant Co. E., April 19, 1862.

W. W. McCRACKEN, Sergeant Major, promoted to 2d Lieutenant Co. A., Nov. 2, 1862.

H. W. NEAL, Quartermaster Sergeant, discharged on Surgeon certificate.

J. G. STEPHENSON, Quartermaster Sergeant, promoted to 2d Lieutenant Co. E., January 28, 1863.

J. K. WILSON, Steward Hospital, died at Holly Springs, Miss., Dec. 24, 1862.

ROSTER TWENTIETH REGIMENT OHIO VETERAN VOLUNTEER INFANTRY.

No.	Names.	Rank.	Date of Commission.	Date of Muster.	Post Office Address.	Remarks.
1	Harry Wilson	Lieut. Colonel	Jan. 11, 1865.	Jan. 27, 1865.	Harrietsville, Ohio	
2	Peter Wetherby	Major	April 1, 1865.	April 25, 1865.	Chesterville, Ohio	
3	H. P. Fricker	Surgeon	Oct. 12, 1864.	Oct. 26, 1864.	Jefferson, Ohio	
4	William L. Waddell	Captain	April 22, 1864.	May 1, 1864.	Mount Vernon, Ohio	Headquarters 3d Div. 17th A. C., S. O. No. 2, Jan. 2, 1865.
5	Reuben M. Colby	"	July 25, 1864.	Sept. 30, 1864.	Sidney, Ohio	
6	Edmund E. Nutt	"	Jan. 10, 1865.	Mar. 25, 1865.	Sidney, Ohio	Headquarters 2d Brig. 3d Div. 17th A. C., S. O. No. 28, May 26, 1865.
7	James E. McCracken	"	Jan. 11, 1865.	Jan. 28, 1865.	Chesterville, Ohio	
8	Newton R. Persinger	"		Jan. 27, 1865.	Sidney, Ohio	
9	Joshua E. Clark	"		Jan. 28, 1865.	Mount Vernon, Ohio	
10	J. C Haines	"			Sidney, Ohio	
11	J. W. Guthrie	Assistant Surgeon	Aug. 20, 1862.	Aug. 20, 1862.	Wooster, Ohio	
12	Henry O. Dwight	1st Lieut. and Adj.	April 23, 1863.	April 23, 1863.	Englewood, N. J.	Headquarters 1st Div. 17th A. C., S. O. No. 72, March 31, 1865.
13	W. H. Nogle	1st Lieutenant	April 24, 1864	May 1, 1864	Dayton, Ohio	
14	John W Skillen	1st Lieut. and R. Q. M.	May 9, 1864.	June 17, 1864.	Sidney, Ohio	Will not accept a Captain's commission.
15	T. L. Hawley	1st Lieutenant	Jan. 11, 1865.	April 10, 1865.	Buck's P. O., Columbiana Co., O.	
16	Chany Grimes	"		Jan. 28, 1865.	Sidney, Ohio	
17	C. W. McCracken	"			Chesterville, Ohio	
18	S. H. Reynolds	"			Sidney, Ohio	
19	William L. Phillips	"			Mount Vernon, Ohio	
20	Jesse S. Felt	"			Mount Vernon, Ohio	
21	Jesse Dickenshuts	"			Sidney, Ohio	
22	George Thoma	"	Feb. 15, 1865.	April 10, 1865.	Gilancy, Knox Co., Ohio	Headquarters 2d Brig. 3d Div. 17th A. C., S. O., No. 19, April 9, 1865.

I certify that the above is a correct Roster of the Regiment.

JESSE S. FELT,

1st Lieut. and Act. Adj. 20th Ohio.

Resolutions of Respect.

WHEREAS, By the wise dispensation of Providence, our beloved country has offered up a sacrifice as an atonement for the national sin of slavery, our freedom has been secured, and our free institutions perpetuated, and our country made a paradise for the nations of the earth to concentrate and enjoy the glorious peace and happiness incident to a pure republic: and,

WHEREAS, It is right and proper that we should reverently cherish a lively recollection of the brave men who offered up their lives upon the bloody battle-field, and those who died from wounds or disease in that gigantic struggle to rescue this nation from the hands of its traitors; and especially do we point with pride to the long list of names herewith submitted, as men who made that sacrifice necessary to complete the work of saving the union:

Resolved, That in the loss of these men we recognize the hand of Providence, and bow with humble submission to His divine will, but deeply mourn the sad fate of them all.

Resolved, That we admire the heroism, the patriotism, and true moral courage of all the dead comrades of the gallant old 20th Ohio Regiment, and the friends and relatives who mourn their loss, we commit to the hands of Him who doeth all things well, begging them to remember the great sacrifice they have made was for the good of their country's cause.

2

Killed and Died in Service.

COMPANY A.

W. H. Roberts............ ......Died.
S. Brollier .... "
P. H. Cosner .... "
A. Davis .... "
L. B. Everats .... "
R. M. Fogle ....Killed.
J. Hayden ....Died.
D. B. Janes ....Killed.
G. M. Ranson ....Died.
B. F. Wilson ....Killed.
H. Williams ....Died.
A. Allison .... "

Z. M. Ball................ ....Died.
Wm. Blackburn .... "
E. Barry................. "
J. Carpenter............ ....Killed.
A. Dyer... ....Died.
C. W. Galliher..... .... "
Dan. Harris.................. "
E. Harris ....Killed.
E. Pollock .... "
A. Skillman .... "
A. J. Strong............... "

COMPANY B.

G. H. Crawford, killed in battle.
W. H. Brown..............Died.
J. Reinhart .... "
Benj. Bailey ....Killed.
G. W. Ragan ....Died.
J. H. Colman .... "
John Johnson ....Killed.
J. C. McAlexander........ "
G. W. Rush............ .....Died.
J. W. Wilson .... "
H. O. Watts .... "
S. Wright .... "
C. Baldwin .... "
D. Baldwin .... "
W. R. Campbell............ "

Levi Gump ....Died.
T. J. Goble................ "
H. P. Hall ....Killed.
A. Hoffman................Died.
T. M. Hall .... "
J. Hashberger............ "
H. D. Much............... "
B. Fogle .... "
G. Pencil .... "
J. S. Schenck .... "
H. Schenck................. "
H. Staley .... "
M. L. Thrush ....Killed.
W. Walters................Died.

COMPANY C.

G. A. Short................Died.
H. A. Stell.................... "
John Patterson.............. "
C. J. Hammon............... "
T. McClure .... "
O. Euely...................... "
W. A. Derby................ "
Isaac Davis ... . "
R. W. Faugh .... "
J. A. Marion................. "
J. R. Noral .... "
G. H. Outen ....Killed.

S. Roseboome............ ......Died.
Lemuel Rightsell ... :.... "
P. B. Varner.............." "
Wm. Miller...... ....Killed.
Ira Davis .... "
Peter Garris............ .....Died.
Henry Mount .... "
Jacob Rothwell .... "
L. W. Reed ....,.....Killed.
Perry Stothart .... "
Joseph Stein................Died.

COMPANY D.

J. W. Dear ....Died.
H. F. Gould.................... "
S. P. Hunter .... "
J. J. Herron ....Killed.
M. D. Haskin.............Died.
Jacob Inskip................ "
Joel Floyd .... "
J. S. McCoy................... "
James R. Snodgrass...... "
J. A. Sabin .... "

Joseph Sills.................Died.
L. C. Shuman ....Killed.
H. Wilson................Died.
J. W. Corwin..............Killed.
J. C. Magfield, died of wounds.
F. Rowley ....Died.
W. P. Smith..............Killed.
E. H. Saunders ....Died.
L. D. Standish.............Killed.

COMPANY E.

Wm. Atherton.............Died.
H. Buzzard .... "
L. C. Baker ....Killed.
W. H. Clark.............Drowned.
E. P. Downs ....Killed.
P. Hirsh ....Died.
J. B. Saunders .... "
A. Lee.................... "
W. F. Myers............... "
A. McClurg................ "
D. Mowery .... "
R. Pickard................. "

O. Watty ....Died.
T. Zimmerman .... "
W. Workman ... . "
J. Cannavan ....Killed.
George M. Long, killed
by explosion of Steamer
Sultana.
H. H. Fulton, died of
wounds.
H. P. Linstead............. "
C. Russell.................. "
G. Skillinger..............Died.

COMPANY F.

W. H. Coy.................Died.
J. Cotterral .... "
Wm. Crothertiller......... "
L. Ellsworth .... "
Wm. Edwards............. "
Wm. Hefflemen .... "
Phillip Hall............... "
Wm. Henman.............. "
Fred. Hines................ "
John Hinsker.............. "
M. Hole................... "
Thos. Jackson.............. "

Thos. Minnear.............Died.
G. Olden.................. "
N. Russell .... "
Wm. Snanger .... "
D. Vanote .... "
J. W. Vandevett.......... "
Elliott Mathias ....Killed.
C. Davenport ....Died.
Robt. Elliott ....Killed.
Albert Hines............... "
John Shaw .... "

COMPANY G.

Enos Milt ....Died.
George L. Mellick......... "
Saml. Davis............... "
J. Bostwick .... "
Caleb Leedy............... "
W. G. Balch.............. "
Wm. Barrible.............. "
J. W. Baxter.............. "

H. H. Lockwood..........Killed.
S. A. Manning............Died.
Isaac McClure .... "
Wm. Newton.............. "
H. Oldaker .... "
J. G. Pitkin............... "
A. Reader................. "
D. F. Snider .... "

12

J. Cochran	Died.	W. C. Smith	Died.
Wm. Cochran	"	J. W. Tathwell	"
Samuel Cochran	"	Esquire Davis	"
George Duncan	"	Romaine White	"
Byron Dean	"	Jacob Waters	"
John Elder	Killed.	James Dunn	"
T. Fitspatrick	Died.	G. M. Cochran	"
Jas. Grimes	"	E. S. Boudinott	"
Calvin C. Hall	"	Joseph White	Killed.
Henry High	"	C. S. Beardsly	"

COMPANY H.

A. Beil	Died.	C. Seebler	Died.
G. Canada	Killed.	H. Shively	Killed.
Sol. Fulk	Died.	Wm. Taylor	"
N. O. Fulk	Killed.	E. M. Quackenbush	Died.
D. E. Huxly	Died.	Joseph Fusselman	"
A. J. Leach	"	Nathan Heminger	Killed.
H. Lawrance	Killed.	Benj. Knox	"
J. McNeally	Died.	Isaac Strock	Died.
N. N. Oviatt	"	Lester C. Robbins	Killed.
F. Richards	"	J. M. Thomas	"
S. Severns	"		

COMPANY I.

D. L. Way	Died.	Wm McClelland	Died.
T. Marion	"	J. W. Newlan	"
G. Archer	"	W. H. Newlan	"
Samuel Beeny	"	H. Nufelt	"
A. Ball	"	H. Parmer	"
Thos. Clogg	"	B. Shakleford	"
S. J. Darling	"	J. M. Wickham	"
A. Englehart	"	W. Wells	"
J. W. Garrett	"	O. Brown	Killed.
R. Hughes	"	E. M. Evans	Died.
J. A. Harbin	"	E. Campbell	Killed.
A. Johnson	"	J. Crow	Died.
P. Johns	"	T. G. Ailes	"
J. King	"	B. Dodds	Killed.
S. Keupp	"	H. J. Harbin	Died.
Wm. Quitt	"	H. O. Reed	Killed.
J. C. Meracle	"	W. Trumble	"
George Mercer	"	Clark Young	Died.
P. Miller	"	A. N. Williams	"
D. Milton	"	W. H. Wickham	"
G. McGugin	"	Peter McBride	"

COMPANY K.

J. W. Andrew	Died.	A. Lenox	Killed.
S. Bryan	"	E. Manning	"

O. P. Bogard..................Died.	M. Stingert ....Killed.
Thos. Baldwin .... "	J. Wagnoy.................... "
C. Bunson .... "	D. C. Baker.................... "
Jesse Babcock..............Killed.	W. D. Neal.................... "
J. O. Cole..................... "	Wm. Argood ....Died.
J. N. Davis .... "	Wm. Dodd.................... "
J. Dalton .... "	Thos. Gleason.............. "
Jesse Day....................... "	C. Jelly....................Killed.
P. Duwese .... "	J. E. Kessler.............. "
E. S. Gallimore .... "	Jas Moore.. .... "
Fr Hankins.................... "	Jasper Miller.............. "
H. Hardisty .... "	John Musshrey .... "
J. A. Knox .... "	Andrew Mills..............Died.
O. Lambort................... "	

Reunion Addresses.

After music by the Mt. Vernon Cornet Band,
D. W. Wood, Chairman, addressed the comrades
as follows :

Ladies, Comrades, and Friends :

This is the first reunion of the 20th Ohio Vete-
ran Volunteer Regiment, after a lapse of nearly
eleven years. Let me assure you that I am su-
premely happy in being selected to preside over
the first reunion of our regiment. I am proud of
being associated with men who stood at their post
of duty during the late civil war, until their country needed their services no longer. I love the
patriotic soldier who left his home and friends for
the bloody battle field when war was raging over
our country, and fought manfully in that gigantic
struggle, to save and perpetuate our glorious Union.

Trusting that this reunion may be soul-cheer-

ing to us all, and in no wise marred by any unchar-
itable sentiment or unbecoming conduct, and that
I shall receive your fraternal assistance and cor-
dial co-operation in all my efforts to conduct your
meeting successfully, we will now proceed to the
regular order of exercises.

The Hon. R. C. Kirk was then introduced, and
delivered the address of welcome. I am sorry he
did not furnish me with a copy of his address, for
this work is incomplete without it. I have to be
content with saying that it was perfectly splendid,
and appropriate for the occasion.

Remarks by General Force.

___

On behalf of the 20th Ohio, I tender to you, sir,
profound thanks for your kind greeting, and to
you, ladies and gentlemen, for your warm welcome.
The survivors of the regiment meet here in their
first reunion since the war. As college graduates
when they assemble at annual meetings, or as the
scattered members of a family when they gather
at some festival in the parental home, talk first of
all of old times when they were young together, so
we to-day instinctively, at sight of each other,
turn back to the times when, in uniforms of blue,
we stood side by side in camp and march and battle. It will not be inappropriate, therefore, to give
a rapid sketch of the history of the regiment, that
you, our hosts, may come to know us better, while
we indulge in reminiscenses of the past.

The field and staff officers were appointed first. Companies were recruited afterwards. Colonel Whittlesey, Major Force and Quartermaster Hitchcock reported at Camp Chase in the latter part of August, 1861, and Company A soon after marched in and was mustered in on the 6th of September. Colonel Whittlesey was soon appointed Engineer in Chief on the staff of General Mitchell, and the regiment recruited under the personal supervision of Lieut. Colonel Force and Major McElroy, at Camp Chase, then Camp Dennison, then in barracks in Cincinnati, then in Camp King, back of Covington, Ky.

While in Camp King, besides daily instruction of schools of officers and non-commissioned officers, drill by squad, company and battalion, and night drills in the woods, details were sent every three days to guard the line of detached earthworks south of Covington and Newport, and Colonel Whittlesey, an experienced regular army officer, took detachments on marches over the country. Colonel Whittlesey, in the autumn, took four companies down the river to Warsaw, Ky., to quell an insurrectionary movement, and when winter came on, the rest of the regiment moved into barracks in Cincinnati.

The 20th, being in the field, was mustered in on the 21st of October, though then little more than half full.

On the 11th of February, 1862, nine companies, leaving Company K to complete its organization, embarked on two small steamers and arrived before Fort Donelson on Friday. Next day the regiment marched to the right of the line and was held in reserve. Sunday morning, when preparing to charge the fort, its surrender was announced.

The 20th was sent north on a fleet of boats, guarding five thousand prisoners of war, and seemed hopelessly scattered. A detachment was left at Fort Donelson, guarding the transportation; a detachment was still at Warsaw; Company K was still at Cincinnati; the rest were at Cairo, St. Louis, Chicago, Columbus and Boston. By the middle of March, seven companies, under Lieut. Colonel Force, rendezvoused at Cairo, and proceeded up the Tennessee river on the Continental, General Sherman's headquarters boat. Continual traveling on boats and cars had so effected the health of the men, that while we lay at Savannah, on the Tennessee, the 20th went by the name of "the sick regiment." But when the sick regiment went out to drill, the rest stopped to look on.

The regiment went with the expedition to Yellow Creek, returned to Pittsburg Landing, and finally, the ten companies being assembled, it was assigned to a brigade, composed of the 20th, 56th, 76th and 78th Ohio, in General Lew Wallace's division, at Crump's Landing, Colonel Whittlesey commanding the brigade, and marched to an advanced post at Adamsville.

Before daylight, Saturday, 5th of April, the brigade formed in line of battle, and General Wallace brought out the rest of the division from Crump's Landing. No attack being made, the rest of the division returned to the Landing. While on Sunday inspection, next day, hearing the cannonade at Shiloh, the regiment was ordered to strike camp and prepare for march. Order to march was given about two o'clock P. M., and after dark we reached the vacant camp of the 81st Ohio. There we lay down on the ground in two ranks, on the slope of the hill, through the night, drenched with rain and listening to the unearthly shrieks of wounded mules and the booming of the naval guns.

In the battle of Monday, the 20th formed the extreme right of the army. While marching into position by the flank, an unseen battery opened on it, but, without pausing, the regiment charged upon it and drove it from the field.

During the advance on Corinth, the 20th was detailed to guard a long exposed line towards Purdy, and upon the evacuation marched through Purdy to Bolivar. It soon moved on to Grand Junction, where Colonel Leggett commanded the 20th, 68th and 78th Ohio, four guns and four companies of cavalry, the command being posted in town, except the 20th, which was encamped separately a mile in advance. This post, twenty-two miles out from Bolivar, isolated, exposed, and continually threatened by cavalry, was held secure by keeping detachments continually on the march scouring the country, until the command was recalled to Bolivar. While camp was at Bolivar, Colonel Leggett's brigade, the 20th and 78th, was incessantly engaged in marches of reconnoissance.

At one o'clock A. M. the 5th of August, the 20th left Bolivar with a supply train for General Ord and General Hurlbut, who had moved to intercept General Price the day before, and, marching twenty-eight miles, reached the battle field at

3

four o'clock P. M., turned over the train, and went out in pursuit of prisoners. Next day, the regiment was sent on a reconnoissance, and returning to camp at sunset, was despatched, without a halt, in company with two other regiments, guarding the prisoners taken in battle to Bolivar.

On the 30th of August, the pickets in front of the brigade reported cavalry in front. A detachment of the 20th was sent out; the brigade followed; four companies of cavalry and two guns were added; and this little force fought all day with the cavalry brigades of Armstrong and Jackson, fifteen regiments strong, till the enemy withdrew at sundown, and the little brigade, all fagged out, dragged itself back to town. This engagement attracted attention at Washington, and Colonel Crocker, commanding at Bolivar, was promoted Brigadier General in recognition of it.

When the movement was made on General Price at Iuka, the 20th moved by rail to Burnesville, and was kept constantly employed in reconnoissance. On the morning of the 20th of September, when General Ord moved on to Iuka, unaware of General Rosecrans' battle of the day before, the regiment was placed at the rear of the column. General Ord sent a staff officer to tell me that the regiment was placed there on account of its hard work for the previous three days, but as soon as the enemy should be met, the 20th should be brought to the front.

When General Grant moved on the 28th of November, from La Grange into Northern Mississippi, General Leggett's brigade was permanently organized as the 2d Brigade of Logan's Division, and comprised the 20th, 68th and 78th Ohio, and 30th Illinois. When the army reached the Yaconapatapa river, the 20th, with two guns, was sent to the front, across the river and the swamp, as advance guard of the army. When the army fell back behind the Tallahatchie, General Leggett's brigade was left south of the river as rear guard to the army, and the 20th was posted by itself a mile beyond the rest of the brigade, as extreme guard.

While lying here, in extreme want of provisions, foraging, which afterwards became an ordinary duty, was resorted to. The 20th and 68th, with a battery, were sent with a train of wagons to a plantation ten miles off, for hogs and corn. Captain George Rogers, of Company E, was detailed to see the lady who owned the plantation. When we were leaving, she said to him, " I know, sir, this is the fate of war, and I can only thank you for the courtesy with which you have performed your duty."

Many of the men were barefooted in the march through rain and snow to Memphis, which was reached on the 28th of January, 1863. Here the 17th Corps was organized, and Logan's division became its 3d Division. The army here prepared for the Vicksburg campaign, though a large part of our occupation was holding courts martial and sitting for photographs. Here was enacted on the picket line the sequel to the famous race to Oxford between the 20th and General Quinby's division.

On the 22d of February, the regiment embarked and sailed down the river to Lake Providence. On the banks of this lake, bordered with great oaks trailing with Spanish moss, in the trim camp, where every tent had a flowering arbor in front, the men led an arcadian life, fishing, bathing, boating and holding evening serenades on the water. But canal digging, and expeditions into the swamps on both sides of the river, gave variety till we moved down to Millikin's Bend, on the 18th of April.

Here the 20th, with the 30th Illinois, was sent out into the swamp to build a road for the army to pass over below Vicksburg. Every day, when the sun went down, the foliage of the trees seemed to dissolve into swarms of gnats ; the earth seemed to smoke up with clouds of gnats, till the night air was a saturated solution of gnats that made breathing difficult, sleep impossible. Here we first met alligators. The first day, a soldier found up a tree by the water's edge, declared that an alligator came at him from the water, with distended jaws, and chased him up the tree.

When the march was begun, and the division came along, the 20th stacked spades, shouldered arms, took its place in the column, and marched to the crossing at Bruinsburg. We reached the field of Port Gibson on the 1st of May, when the battle was over. Colonel Dennis, of the 30th Illinois, promoted Brigadier General, commanded the Brigade until the day of the battle of Champion Hill, when Colonel Leggett returned from the north, also a Brigadier General, and resumed command. While General Dennis commanded, though the other regiments shifted position every day, the 20th was always kept in the front, at the head of the brigade.

On the 3d of May, General McPherson, observing signs of the enemy, deployed the corps and moved cautiously. The 2d Brigade was detached and sent to the left towards Grand Gulf. Making a detour of twenty miles, the brigade came out in front of the corps, which had meanwhile advanced four miles, and then the 20th, making a dash for the Big Black river, drove off a party of the enemy who were destroying a temporary bridge across the river at Hankinson's Ferry, and prevented its destruction.

On the 12th, the 20th deployed as skirmishers in front of the 17th Corps, as it approached Raymond. While lying at a halt in the timber, by Fourteen Mile creek, the forest suddenly rang with a yell and a volley. The 20th sprang forward into the creek, using its bank for a breastwork. The fire was so close that at times muskets crossed, and some men who were shot were burnt with the powder. The line gave way to the right, and the enemy there pushed on to the rear of the 20th. The regiment held its place till the line was reformed, and then charged. When the battle was over, and the corps marched into Raymond, the 20th was advanced beyond the town as reserve to the pickets for the night. In the course of the battle, Lieutenant Stevenson, commanding Company E, was severely wounded, and First Sergeant Selby, whose commission as Lieutenant was then on the way from Ohio, was killed, leaving the company in command of Fifth Sergeant Oldroyd, who had been appointed only a few days before. He was so ably seconded by Private John Conovan, that Conovan was appointed Sergeant on the field.

On the day of the battle of Jackson, the 20th was detailed to guard the train from an expected attack. At the beginning of the battle of Champion Hill, the regiment lay in line at the foot of the hill, exposed to a dropping fire, while General McPherson was extending the line to the right. When command was given, the regiment charged up the hill and drove the opposing line into the woods. It took position in a ravine, where the fire was so hot that staff officers could hardly approach with orders. A massed column moved towards our line. The two regiments adjoining the 20th recoiled a space, but the 20th, with ammunition nearly gone, fixed bayonets and stood with steel bristling above the bank in their front, till the 68th Ohio came up in support, bringing ammunition. When the battle was over, we marched several miles beyond the field before going into bivouac for the night.

The 20th was in place in the line investing Vicksburg, in the earlier part of the siege, but marched in General Blair's reconnoissance up the Yazoo to Patastia, and afterwards formed part of General Sherman's army of observation, watching General Johnston. When the siege was over, we marched out to the siege of Jackson, and then returned to rest.

After the termination of the siege of Vicksburg, a Board of Honor was appointed by General McPherson, to award medals of honor to officers and soldiers in the corps who had distinguished themselves by acts of special gallantry, in the war up to that time. The following awards were made to the Twentieth Ohio: Gold medals to Brigadier

General M. F. Force, as Colonel of the regiment, and Private Mathias Elliott, of Company F ; silver medals to Captain Lyman N. Ayres, Captain Harrison Wilson, Sergeant John Rinehart, of Company B ; Sergeant David Robbins, of Company F, and Private John Alexander, of Company D.

While lying about Vicksburg, the 20th formed part of General Stevenson's expedition to Monroe, Louisiana, and, later, of General McPherson's reconnoissance towards Canton.

The 20th re-enlisted as veterans, marched in General Sherman's raid to Meridian, and, on the return, went home on the veterans' furlough.

When the furlough expired, the regiment rendezvoused at Camp Dennison, on the 1st of May, 1864, proceeded to Cairo, thence by steamers up the Tennessee to Clifton, and marching thence two hundred and fifty miles, by Pulaski, Huntsville, Decatur and Rome, joined Sherman's army, on the 9th of June, at Ackworth. The 20th, for a while, guarded the trains, but rejoined the brigade at Bushy Ridge, at the foot of Kenesaw, on the 23d of June, and took part in the demonstration made on the 27th, by General Leggett, on the extreme right of the enemy's line, while the army made the assault on Kenesaw.

Upon the evacuation of Kenesaw, General Leggett's division, including the 20th, was shifted from the extreme left to the extreme right of the army, and operated about the mouth of Nickajack creek, till it crossed the Chattahoochie on the 16th of July, and took position again on the extreme left flank.

On the 21st of July, the First Brigade of the division took by assault a fortified bald hill, defended by a portion of Coburn's famous division, in full view of Atlanta, in easy range of the guns defending the city. In the course of the day, the Second Brigade moved up into line with the First. The Fourth Division, just come under the command of Giles A. Smith, in consequence of the wounding of General Gresham, moved up later, extending the line to the left.

Next day, about noon, General Hood having moved out from Atlanta with his army, fell furiously upon Giles A. Smith's exposed flank, and part of his force passing around, attacked General Leggett's division from the rear. The men leaped over the works to the side next to Atlanta, and repelled the assault. A new force coming up from the Atlanta side, the men again leaped their works and repelled this new assault. The first column having rallied, returned the assault, and, the men again leaping over their works, repelled them again. Giles A. Smith's division being now rolled up by the flank attack, the force opposing him moved up, and planting guns at close range, enfiladed our line. Fortunately, the men had spent the night in building traverses to their breastworks. Attacked on three sides, the division concentrated on the position held by the First Brigade, and there fought into the night, hand to hand, with bayonets, clubbed muskets, and officers using their swords. Desperate were the contests about the regimental colors, and for the possession of ammunition boxes.

At one time, a squad of two dozen men, with

the colors of the 20th and 78th, charged upon the enemy's line and rescued a number who had been taken prisoners. In this charge, the color bearer of the 78th was killed. Before the colors touched the ground, they were seized and borne by Private Elliott, of Company F of the 20th. In a moment he was killed. His brother, of the same company, snatched them from falling. He, too, was at once killed, and then Private   , also of the same company, took the colors and brought them safely back to the works. In another charge, made by a small party to rescue some boxes of ammunition, Private Blackburn, of Company A, was bayoneted in the hand, but knocked down his assailant with his fist, shouldered a box of cartridges and brought them back to the regiment.

In the night, exhaustion ended the conflict. The hill, afterwards called Leggett's Hill, was held. A brigade took it on the 21st, an army failed to retake it on the 22d.

The morning of the 23d found the hill literally piled up with dead. Corpses lay in heaps. From a portion of the ground fought over by his division, General Leggett buried and turned over by flag of truce, nearly one thousand of the enemy's dead.

For special gallantry in this battle, gold medals of honor were awarded by the Board of the 17th Corps, to Lieutenant Nutt, of Company F, and Private Blackburn, of Company A.

The division was again moved around to the right flank of the army. The 20th, for a time, guarded the trains, but was again in line at the battle of Jonesboro, and at Lovejoy's Station.

4

After remaining in camp a while after the evacuation of Atlanta, the 20th took part in the pursuit of General Hood, as far as Gaylorsville, Alabama, and returned to camp near Marietta.

On the 15th of November, the army launched out upon an expedition, facing towards the east, and was embarked on the march to the sea. Railroads were destroyed, swamps were traversed, rivers were bridged, and the outposts of Savannah were reached. On the 19th of December, the 20th was detached to build wharves on the Ogeechee, for the landing of stores, and was so occupied when Savannah surrendered.

On the 5th of January, 1865, the regiment moved by boat to Beaufort, and before daylight of the 14th, crossed with the 2d Brigade over a pontoon bridge, from the upper end of the island to the main land, followed by the rest of the 17th Corps. The brigade marched at the head of the column, brushing away opposing cavalry, till the advance was stopped by heavy field works on the farther side of a bayou. The 1st Brigade, making a detour, and driving back opposing cavalry, forced the crossing of another bayou, and penetrated to the rear of the works. The skirmish line of the 20th, led by Colonel Wilson, taking the opportunity, dashed at the works, and the force defending them withdrew.

The main column, with the 2d Brigade at its head, resumed the march, and by sunset reached the front of the formidable and often attacked, but hitherto impregnable, works near Pocotalijo.

These works were abandoned in the night, and next day the 20th moved on beyond Pocotalijo, and aided in throwing up works to be held by General Foster's command, when Sherman's army should proceed on its march.

The march was begun by the 17th Corps, on the 30th of January. On the 2d of February, when Generals Mower and Smith crossed Whippy Swamp, near its junction with the Tallahatchie, the 3d Division moved along the borders of the swamp to Barker's Mills, where it becomes a creek, in order to save the bridge at that point, in anticipation of the arrival of the 15th Corps. The march was opposed, but not impeded, by cavalry. The crossing was reached just after sunset. The skirmishers of the 20th waded in, but found the stream too deep to be forded. The 20th lined the shore with their fire, while the 78th dashed across the bridge, supported by the 15th Ohio battery, which, posted on a rising ground, fired over their heads. Next day, the division turned over the bridge, uninjured, to the 15th Corps, on its arrival, and rejoined the 17th Corps, forcing the bloody crossing of the Tallahatchie.

On the morning of the 11th of February, the division, with the 20th in front, moved from the South Fork of the Edisto, with orders to push for the North Fork of the Edisto, opposite Orangeburg, and save the bridge from destruction, but not to cross over. The division coming up about noon to the edge of the swamp through which the Edisto flows in many channels, and to which the opposing cavalry had been driven by our cavalry and foragers, the 20th was detached and pushed into the swamp at a double quick, driving the cavalry so rapidly as to save the causeway and the bridges over the swollen channels to a bend in the road near the last bridge, over the principal channel. This bridge was commanded by a battery, which opened as soon as the cavalry crossed, and the 20th, drawn from the road, was posted along the border of the main stream, in the edge of the timber, standing knee-deep and hip-deep in the water, so as to cover the bridge with their rifles.

In the afternoon, Colonel Wiles, of the 2d Brigade, found the river a mile above, subdivided into a greater number of channels, so that by fording, and by felling trees, men could get over. A party sent by Colonel Fairchild, commanding the 1st Brigade, found that, a mile below, the river was concentrated into one stream, with solid ground on our side, and bordered by swamp on the farther side. When I went in the evening to report this to General Blair, General Sherman and General Howard were with him. As soon as I finished, General Sherman said at once to General Blair, "Yes, the lower place is the place to cross. Make your crossing there, your feint at the bridge, your diversion above."

In the night the enemy threw some pitch on the bridge, and set fire to it, burning some of the planking but not injuring the timbers. In the night, the 3d Division, relieved by Giles Smith, left the position about the bridge, and constructed a road to the proposed crossing.

Next morning a pontoon bridge was constructed at the proposed crossing, the division passed over, waded through the swamp, and emerged into a long stretch of fields that extended to the city. The 2d Brigade was sent by a by-road to cut the railroad below the city, while the 1st Brigade marched on to the battery that was still firing across the river at Giles Smith. The fire was turned on the brigade, but on its approach the guns were limbered up and hurried off. As the brigade was ascending the slope to the town, an officer and three men of Giles Smith's division, clambered over the stringers of the burned bridge and entered the city in company with the brigade. The bridge was repaired and Giles Smith and Mower, with the trains, crossed over it. Orangeburg was strongly held and an obstinate resistance was expected, but only the skirmish line was able to fire on the railway train that took towards Columbus the last of the garrison.

On the evening of the 15th, the 20th and 68th Ohio, under Colonel Wiles, forced the crossing of Congaree creek, at Taylor's bridge, wading the creek, and in the night rebuilt the bridge. The force that was opposing the 15th Corps at Congaree creek, being flanked by this movement, withdrew next morning and left the passage unopposed.

The 20th reached position near Bentonville, on the afternoon of the 19th of March, entrenched next day, and the enemy withdrew on the night of the 20th. On the 24th of March, the regiment moved into Goldsborough, ragged, barefooted and hungry, but in jubilant spirits, confident in its invincibility, and ready, after a two weeks' rest, to march wherever the army commander should direct.

In this march of fifty-four days, there was not much fighting, but there was terrible toil.

General Joe. Johnston often told General Sherman that his Engineers had reported it was a mere impossibility for an army train to pass over the lower portion of South Carolina in the winter, and he did not dream the attempt would be made. The loose soil, nowhere solid, the abundance of swamps, the frequent rain melting the earth away, afforded no foundation for two thousand loaded wagons, besides batteries, ambulances and saddle horses.

The roads were given up to wheels; the troops made their own roads along side. The wagons were, of course, continually sticking and mired to the hubs. It was necessary all the while, to build corduroy road for the wagons, besides constructing ways for the troops. All the divisions were employed in this way. The amount of this work done by the 3d Division, while making this march of four hundred and thirty-two miles, made in the aggregate: 15 miles, 1353 yards of corduroy road for wagons; 122 miles, 627 yards of side road for troops, 303 yards of small bridges where pontoons could not be used; 1 mile, 520 yards of infantry intrenchments, besides erecting a battery for two guns and another for three guns, and destroying, 14 miles, 800 yards of railway, heating and twisting spirally every rail. The toilsome dragging through the mud continually, prolonged the march into the night. For days and nights together, the division was on the road day and night, till the men were haggard for want of sleep.

After two weeks of rest and preparation at Goldsboro, the army, exhilarated with the news of the surrender of Richmond, moved out for Raleigh, and on the way, while floundering in a swamp, heard borne swiftly along the column, the announcement of the surrender of Lee. While pausing at Raleigh, the army sat one day in their tents, silent in the gloom of grief and brooding wrath upon the tidings of the death of Lincoln. Another day, when just stretched out on the road to resume the march, they were crazed with joy by the proclamation of the final surrender of Johnston and the close of the war.

The work was done. Nothing was left but to march home and cast aside the trappings of war. On the route from Raleigh to Washington, the veterans moved easily and rapidly over solid ground. Though Sherman's army, sixty thousand bummers, poured along the country roads, not a chicken started in alarm, the grunting pigs lay still and winked in lazy security at the tramping columns. For peace had come. The rights of war were laid. It was a column of sixty thousand farmers traveling along their brothers' farms, and property was sacred.

The army passed in review at Washington, and tarried awhile at Louisville. The 20th left Louisville on the 15th of July, for Camp Chase, for the final muster out, and all the paraphernalia of war melted away like storm clouds before the sun, leaving the sky of peace to bless us all.

From the time of the muster-in of the first company at Camp Chase, to the final muster-out, was four years, lacking little more than a month. From the time of the arrival of the regiment before Fort Donelson, to the surrender of General Johnston, was more than three years. For the greater part of this time, I had the fortune to be associated with the regiment, either as one of its officers, or as commander of the brigade or division in which it served. During the whole of the time of which I can speak from personal knowledge, after its entering into actual service, it was continuously in the field, on active duty, at the extreme front, and a great part of the time in exposed situations. But the 20th Ohio was never taken by surprise, was never thrown into confusion, never gave back under fire ; it took every point it was ordered to take, and held every position it was ordered to hold.

The instruction of Colonel Whittlesey, in the beginning of our service, in using all practicable cover in battle, saved many lives. According to the muster rolls in Columbus, sixty-two of the regiment were killed and two hundred and eighteen died of wounds and disease while in the service. How many of the discharged went home to die, and how many have died since the war of their wounds, we have no means of knowing. But when we think of Colonel Fry, and Colonel McElroy, and Captain Walker, Captain Ayres, Captain Edwards, Lieutenant Hale and the many others we can name, we shrink from the count. But Colonel Whittlesey, the father of the regiment, thank God, still lives and is with us here to-day. And General Leggett, who, as the 20th and 78th were wedded during the war, is our father-in-law, thank God, still lives and is with us here to-day. And a goodly number of the regiment, who show by their lives that true soldiers in war make trusty citizens in peace, thank God, still live and are gathered here to-day.

The narrative is now ended. But before closing I desire to say one or two things in general, which apply not only to the 20th Ohio, but as well to the army of which it formed a part.

I have often heard it said that the western army was wanting in discipline. And it is true that in the matter of salutes, of forms of respect, all those things that constitute what may be called military etiquette, and which are undoubtedly an important branch of discipline, the western army was deficient. Our military education was hurried, and many things were never learned. But in the vital matter of discipline, in that which constitutes its soul and essence, in unquestioning obedience of orders, the western army was not behind any. If an order was disregarded, the unfortunate recusant suffered.

In the autumn of 1862, a division, moving out of Bolivar to begin a march, was slow and irregular in getting on the road. The division commander was relieved and sent home. On the march, orders were sent out every night specifying the hour at which the march would be resumed in the morning, and we moved by the minute hand of the watch. One morning, in Georgia, a brigade was not ready at the appointed time; another brigade took its place. That night an order was issued disbanding the brigade and assigning the regiments to other brigades. At the beginning of the march from Atlanta to Savannah, a general order was published, prohibiting soldiers from entering any house, except on order of an officer. One day, when the column was lying at rest at a halt, a soldier stepped to a house and stood awhile in the doorway without going farther. At that night's camp, he was tried by regimental court-martial and sentenced to a stoppage of pay. Another soldier, who entered a house and pillaged some article, and an article of trifling value, was tried by general court-martial when we reached Savannah, and sentenced to death.

But were not Sherman's bummers proof of a want of discipline? They are here to speak for themselves. They were the foragers of the army. The trains could not carry sufficient supplies. On setting out on the march from Pocotalijo, that lasted fifty-four days, the 3d division, for example, took twenty-eight days of hard bread, thirty days of coffee, and some sugar and salt. The wagons and haversacks could carry no more. Some cattle were taken along, but not a pound of meat was taken in the wagons. To live on the country was a necessity, a mere matter of course. An invading army always subsists partially or wholly upon the country over which it passes. Napoleon, in his maxims, discusses the relative merits of drawing subsistence by requisition and drawing it by direct seizure. In the densely inhabited countries of Europe, the alternative exists. But in our sparsely settled States, where towns are few and small and scantily supplied, and provisions are mainly found on the scattered plantations, there is no means but direct seizure.

Foragers were a necessity. Every morning, an officer and a squad of men from every regiment, regularly detailed and mounted, were sent out to scour the country and bring in supplies. They commonly went 10, sometimes 20 miles off from the line of march. By intelligence that seemed instinct, they divined where the column would halt for the night. Gathering there, they observed the staff officers indicate the ground for divisions and brigades, and each squad knowing the position of its regiment in the brigade line, unloaded at the spot where their comrades were to arrive. And so the troops that reached camp before morning, found camp fires burning for them, and supplies for supper on the ground.

These foragers, spreading like a cloud over the country, veiled the progress of the column. Whenever they heard a shot, they at once hastened to the spot. If any squad was attacked, help soon came. If they were pressed back, they continually grew stronger by concentration, till they could repel whatever force attacked them. So the infantry tugged their wagons through the roads undisturbed. General Sherman told me that General Johnston said to him: " Your foragers were the most efficient light cavalry ever known. They covered your flanks so completely that I could never penetrate through them far enough to feel your column. And the fact that they could be sent so far off from the eyes of the commanding officers, and return regularly at night, is proof of the highest state of discipline in your army."

Comrades of the 20th Ohio, the four years we spent together—four years sparkling with fun, yet tremulous with pathos, laden with anguish, ennobled with high purpose and lofty resolve—teem with memories that are interwoven with the very texture of our hearts. We could as soon forget the hours of our childhood ; we could as soon forget our mothers' love, as forget the ties that bound us to each other. Yet we pray those years may never return. We pray this land may be free from civil strife forever more.

War is essentially cruel. Its purpose is destruction. Like the surgeon practicing his profession, the soldier, in the progress of war, finds his sensibility grow dull to inevitable suffering. War grows more relentless the longer it lasts. It is simply horrible if not undertaken for some worthy end. But when begun from principle, and carried on from duty to enforce a sacred right, war is consecrated; it calls into action all that is noblest and best in man, and affords some compensation for its calamities.

Who can count the hearts that bled? Who can number the homes that mourned? Yet every man who gave his life a willing sacrifice for us and for his country, by showing us how to die instructed us how we should live. And every woman who, in her errand of mercy, gave her life to save the lives of others, blessed the earth like an angel visitant from higher spheres. And while the war strode across the land like a tornado, scattering havoc and devastation, yet, like a tornado, it dispelled the miasma that was poisoning our system. We were one nation living under one government; but the two sections, opposed in their institutions, were continually growing asunder, divergent and alienated. The war swept away the cause of difference, and left us not only one in nationality and one in government, but one in institutions. This generation must bear the suffering and wear the scars, but posterity will reap the benefit.

Comrades, we no more camp and march and battle side by side. Our homes are widely scattered; we follow diverse pursuits ; we worship in various churches ; we vote in different parties; but we still are one in declaring that the war must not be in vain; its results shall stand; this nation shall be forever one ; its laws shall be obeyed, and the government saved at so great cost, shall be administered with such honor and purity as to justify the cost of saving it. But we cannot ask of others what we fail ourselves to do. It is the duty of every man, above all it is the duty of every soldier who served in the war, to show in his own life an example of that obedience to law and purity of character that we demand in others. See to it that this great land is the home of a nation truly great; and when the next centennial year rolls around, posterity, while honoring the founders of the Republic, may have some kind words for those who saved it in its sorest peril.

CINCINNATI, 15th April, 1876.

CAPT. D. W. WOOD—*Dear Sir:* Your letter of yesterday, just received, gave me quite a start. I have been at the court-house until eleven o'clock or later, every night since I returned from Mt. Vernon, and have not been able to do anything whatever. I did not feel troubled, however, as I understood you to say you would not need the manuscript for two or three weeks. I will at once find some time to put my manuscript in order, or else send it to you in disorder.

The photograph came in good order, and is an excellent picture. I should like to have a copy of the photo. of the regiment, and of the three colonels. I think the picture is better when taken directly from the negative without being retouched.

If you could take the trouble to let me know the price of them, I should be glad to send it, together with my contribution towards the cost of printing the pamphlet.

I have thought over what a capital time we had at Mt. Vernon.
I have been at larger military re-unions, and more elaborate, but
never at one that was more thoroughly enjoyable, or where the
preparations were more complete or the hospitality more warm
and graceful.   Truly, yours,   M. F. FORCE.

Address of Col. Chas. Whittlesey,

April 6, 1876.

*To the Surviving Members of the 20th Regiment Ohio
Volunteers:*

I have met very few of you since we parted on
the battle ground of Shiloh, in the latter part of
April, 1862.

Our separation at that time, was the result of
circumstances that were imperative. I am confident that any of you would have made the same
decision under the same circumstances.

To me, the separation was decidedly painful.
On my part, the letter addressed to you on that
memorable morning, expressed only in a brief and
formal way, my personal attachment to the regiment. [* See copy attached hereto.] I felt for
the officers and men of the command a sincere respect and regard, which to this hour has not become less. It was with great reluctance I accepted
the position of Colonel in the volunteers, very
much preferring the place and duty of a Military
Engineer. I knew that you were citizens, in all
respects my equals, enlisting in the war from mo-
tives of patriotism, before the days of bounties

and conscriptions. I was also conscious that
without discipline, you would never aid much in
the accomplishment of what you all wished to ac-
complish, the destruction of the rebellion. But I
had an instinctive dread of the effects of the se-
verity of camp life, coming as you did from com-
fortable homes and social surroundings. We
were personally strangers to each other. Most of
the companies came from portions of the State
where I was not acquainted. With one exception,
each company was from different counties, and
were strangers to each other. Companies coming
into Camp Chase, assigned to me, were frequently
directed to other regiments. It was a long time
before the regiment was full, and before we got
acquainted with each other. The more I perceived among the men and officers a high grade of
intelligence, the more I dreaded the effects of discipline upon you. I found myself in command of
nearly a thousand mechanics, farmers, lawyers,
physicians and merchants ; but the question
weighed incessantly upon my mind—what kind of
soldiers will they make ? Many of you, at home,
were men of business position and property, and
the great query was, when the day of battle shall
come, how will they fulfill their duty as soldiers ?
But these were useless apprehensions. I soon
found you had a good set of officers, which was a
great relief. The Adjutant, Lieutenant Owens ;
Quartermaster, Lieutenant Hitchcock, were of my
own selection. Their subsequent conduct justified
all that I expected of them. The field officers,
Lieutenant Colonel Force and Major James McElroy, came into the regiment by assignment, but I

could not have done better if I had appointed them myself. I found the Captains and subalterns were of a much higher order than I had reason to expect. They went to work harmoniously, perfecting the discipline of their men, who took to it much more kindly than I expected. I had not then learned the lesson that soldiers, in a patriotic war, may be made valuable just in proportion to their intelligence.

A portion of my time was still occupied in engineering duty, and work perfecting the command fell largely upon the other officers.

When we moved into the lines opposite Cincinnati, in October, 1861, the troubles I had anticipated from the vicinity of grog-shops, were not realized. The men appeared to have a personal self-respect as citizens and an ambition to do their duty as soldiers.

In constructing the defences of Covington, I needed mechanics as well as laborers, and found no difficulty in getting details from the regiment, who could do every kind of work and do it willingly.

When we were ordered down the river into Kentucky, as a police force over the counties of Boone, Owen, Carroll and Gallatin, your conduct there raised you still higher in my estimation. I began to entertain a feeling of confidence. But, as yet, you were untried in battle. No one can foresee how he will acquit himself, when he meets the enemy for the first time. A persistent battle is the highest expression of human courage and energy. The first conflict is the greatest occasion of a lifetime. Whoever passes this ordeal creditably, rises in his own estimation. If he fails, it is never forgotten by himself or his fellow-men.

In February, 1862, we were ordered to Paducah, subject to orders from General Grant. Arriving there on transports, we were turned about instantly, to join the investment of Fort Donelson. Just as the sun was setting, on the 14th, our boats reached the landing, a couple of miles below where the fleet, under Commodore Foote, was bombarding the fort. Taking Adjutant Owens, I rode out to the lines for orders, through the mud and snow.

We found the headquarters about dark, with no one present but an orderly. In a short time, General Grant and staff returned, assigning us to the right of the line, under McClernand, with orders to remain on the transports till morning.

You probably remember the parade at daylight, in a frozen cornfield, and the march over an execrable route in search of McClernand. About 10 o'clock A. M., his division was pretty much disorganized by the rebel attack of that morning. General McClernand could not be found, and I reported to General Lew Wallace, who commanded the centre. His orders were to go in, as soon as Colonel Wood's regiment, the 76th Ohio, had exhausted their ammunition. The moment had arrived for which all our drill and discipline had been only the preparation. We were surrounded by circumstances very trying to new troops. We lay in a thick wood, on an old road, over which the artillery passed to the front. Round shot from the fort was cutting off the limbs of the trees over our heads. An Illinois regiment lay on the opposite side of the road, ducking their heads as the shot whizzed through the leafless trees. Their Colonel came rushing up the road, saying that Schwartz' battery was captured, Taylor's had only twenty-eight horses left, and Waterhouse could hold out but little longer. The wounded were being brought along the road to the rear, their blood dripping through their blankets on the snow. Colonel Logan sat on his horse, wounded in the shoulder, suffering intensely, waiting for a surgeon. A heavy cannonade was going on not far to the front, at the edge of the timber. The Chicago Board of Trade Battery was ordered forward at a gallop. In passing us, a gun upset and caught a man under it, which nearly killed him. It was a trying moment for me, also, conscious that even veterans might not move promptly into line amid all those discouragements. Colonel Woods' regiment was sent in; the Chicago battery righted its gun and went forward with a rush.

Standing in the bushes, I could not see more than two or three of our companies at a time. Riding along the line from the right, I called each company to attention, giving it special instructions what to do. I could look into the upturned face of every man, as they listened to my directions. When I reached the last company, every doubt had vanished. I experienced a new sensation of mingled pride, confidence and power. In the "Wandering Jew," I had read of a General of the Jesuits, who had been a Colonel of Cavalry, relating how he felt when his regiment had proven itself in a charge. No one can appreciate this emotion who has not been through his experience. He thought himself magnified into a thousand men. Beside the idea of power, I experienced a lofty military pride in the command of such men. I felt an assurance that you would go anywhere that I would go myself, and if we should fail of success and be repulsed, it would not be until the number of the dead would be such as to consecrate the spot in after times.

But the order was soon changed from a movement direct to the front, to one on the right, forming a crotchet against a presumed advance of the enemy in pursuit of McClernand. This was the last order I received, until the morning of the surrender, when General Grant directed me to take charge of the prisoners. We slept that night among the same regiments from Illinois, who had borne themselves so bravely in the fight of the morning. Quartermaster Hitchcock had brought up a few teams with rations, which we shared with those men, who were hungry and had become veterans in a day. You were thus initiated into the realities of war. The next trial was at Shiloh, then at Corinth, and the march to Grenada, to Vicksburg, Champion Hill, Atlanta and the sea, upon which General Force has already discoursed. I wish to add, however, that I had frequent reports of your behavior in these marches and in the battles I have named. You were always on my mind —my interest in your reputation was equal to your own.

From the day of our separation to this, I know of nothing that abates the confidence and the regard that flashed upon me on that morning at Donelson.

General Force has said to me, in his correspondence, that every order you received was not only executed, but within the time named in the order. I do not see how any higher praise can be given to a regiment and to the officers and men who compose it.

---

* Parting Correspondence.

CAMP SHILOH, TENN., April 20, 1862.

To the Officers and Men of the 20th Reg. O. Vol.:

I have found it necessary to offer my resignation, which, having been accepted, I now retire from the service.

Before separating myself from you, I wish to express my general satisfaction with the conduct of the regiment. Wherever you have been stationed, the citizens in the vicinity have voluntarily commended your demeanor toward them, your sobriety and your intelligence. I did not suppose it possible to place so many men under the restraint of military life, with so little difficulty. This is owing to the fact that the best citizens, those who are the most respectable and orderly, make the best soldiers. They submit to discipline from principle, rather than from fear of punishment. I have taken pride in the command of such men, and felt confident that when the hour of battle arrived, you would do your whole duty, as you have done. I owe very much of this result to the assiduity and capacity of the field officers of

the regiment and the regimental staff. Having
been much of the time on detached service, without this hearty co-operation, you might not have
been so well prepared for effective service. The
same may be said of the commissioned officers
generally. There has also been unusual personal
harmony among the officers of all grades.

The non-commissioned officers, too, have won
my esteem by the fidelity and alacrity with which
they have performed their duties.

I wish to say further, that I remember no instance of insolent or disrespectful language being
used toward myself by any officer or man in the
regiment.

I part from you with regret, having full confidence that you will continue cheerfully to submit
to discipline, and will never disgrace your present
reputation; that when this infamous rebellion is
broken up, as it soon will be, you will return to
your homes and become good citizens, where you
will be repaid for your toils, by the respect of your
neighbors and friends. There you will enjoy
through life the proud consciousness of having
given your best efforts in support of the most
righteous and important cause for which ever men
fought.   CHAS. WHITTLESEY,
            Col. 20th Reg. Ohio Volunteers.

———

CAMP SHILOH, }
NEAR PITTSBURG LANDING, TENN., }
April 21st, 1862. }

COL. CHAS. WHITTLESEY—*Sir:* We deeply
regret that you have resigned the command of the
20th Ohio. The considerate care evinced for the

soldiers in camp, and above all, for the courage, coolness and prudence displayed on the battle-field, have inspired officers and men with the highest esteem for, and most unbounded confidence in, you as our commander.

From what we have seen at Fort Donelson, and at the bloody field near Pittsburg, on Monday, the 7th, all felt ready to follow you unfalteringly into any contest, and into any post of danger. While giving expression to our unfeigned sorrow at your departure from us, and assurance of our high regard and esteem for you, and unwavering confidence as our leader, we would follow you with the earnest hope that your future days may be spent in uninterrupted peace and quiet, enjoying the happy reflections and richly earned rewards of well spent service in the cause of our blessed country in its dark hour of need.

Your obedient servants,

MANNING F. FORCE, *Lt. Colonel,*
JAMES N. McELROY, *Major 20th Regt.*

P. M. Hitchcock, *Qr. Master.*   E. A. Owen, *Adjutant.*

John C. Fry, Capt. Co. B.   George Rogers, Capt. Co. E.
J. M. McCoy, " C.   Chas H. McElroy, " D.
A. Kaga, " K.   Wm. H. Updegraff, " F.
T. M. Shaklee, " I.   E. C. Downs, " H.
William Rogers, " A.   B. A. T. Grier, 1st Lt. Co. E.
V. T. Hills, 1st Lt. Co. D.   I. L. Meleck, " G.
A. J. Edwards, " B.   Lyman N. Ayres, " A.
Harrison Wilson, " I.   E. Garis, " C.
Henry M. Davis, 2d Lt. Co. H.   D. B. Rhinehard, 2d Lt. Co. K.
W. H. Jacobs, " E.   R. M. Colby, " B.
W. L. Waddel, " I.   G. Hale, " B.
P. Weatherby, " A.   Robert I. Irwin, " C.
Henry O. Dwight, " H.   William D. Neal, " F.

47

CINCINNATI, OHIO, Nov. 20, 1861.

Maj. Gen. HALLECK, *St. Louis:*

SIR: Will you allow me to suggest the consideration of a great movement by land and water, up the Cumberland and Tennessee rivers?

1st. Would it not allow of water transportation half way to Nashville?

2d. Would it not necessitate the evacuation of Columbus, by threatening their railway communication?

3d. Would it not necessitate the retreat of Gen. Buckner, by threatening his railway lines?

4th. Is it not the most feasible route into Tennessee?

Yours, respectfully,

CHAS. WHITTLESEY,
Col. Chief Engineer Dept. of Ohio.

WAR DEP'T, ADJ. GEN'L OFFICE, Dec. 11, 1875.

Official paper.

L. H. PELOUZE,
Asst. Adjt. Gen.

CLEVELAND, O., April 24, 1876.

Capt. D. W. WOOD:

DEAR SIR—I have just returned from Boston, Mass., and find your favor of the 14th inst. I will, if possible, get time to reduce my "ramblings" at Mt. Vernon to writing; but don't delay a moment for me, for I greatly fear I shall have no time at my control. I doubt whether what I said has any place, properly, in your proposed publication.

Very Truly, &c.,

M. D. LEGGETT.

SIDNEY, O., May 10, 1876.

Capt. WOOD, *Mt. Vernon, O.:*

MY DEAR SIR—I think it impossible to give for publication, anything like a correct report of my random speeches made at our reunion. My business engagements have been such, that I could not give my early attention to your request, and now everything has faded from memory. I am unwilling to have reported and circulated anything different from what I said, which might look like an afterthought, or attempt to improve for the purpose. I don't think the proceedings will lose interest by leaving my efforts out, or by merely mentioning them incidentally, as you will have too much other matter too voluminous to report. Let me beg of you that you will adopt this course, and excuse me.

Respectfully, etc.,

H. WILSON.

HEADQUARTERS 20th REG'T, O. VOLUNTEER INFANTRY,
SNYDER'S BLUFF, MISS., June 3d, 1863.
Brig. Gen'l CHARLES W. HILL, *Adjutant General of O.:*

GENERAL—I have the honor to report the following list of casualties in the 20th Regiment, Ohio Volunteer Infantry, in the action near Raymond, Miss., May 12th, 1863:

Company A, Killed—Privates Joseph Carpenter and Ephraim Harris.

Wounded—Privates Thomas B. Runyon, head, mortally; George Hoover, hand, slightly.
Missing—none.

Company B, Killed—Private Martin L. Thrush.
Wounded—Corporals James Hashburger, chest, mortally, since died; Wm. H. Brown, mouth, slightly; Jonathan Rea, hand, slightly.
Missing—none.

Company C, Killed—Private Strander Raseboom.
Wounded—Privates Patrick Nugent, arm, slightly; John C. Simmons, hand, slightly; Wm. Bevridge, thigh, slightly.
Missing—none.

Company D, Killed—Private Lyman C. Sherman.
Wounded—Corporal Amos C. Mount, hand, slightly; Privates Chancy W. Smith, hand, slightly; Edward Allen, arm slightly; Stephen P. Thrall, body, slightly; Frank Pierson, shoulder, slightly.
Missing—none.

Company E, Killed—1st Sergeant Byron Selby; Private Leroy C. Baker.
Wounded—2d Lieutenant John G. Stevenson, neck, severely; Corporals John C. Wooddell, head, mortally, since died; Abram Frazier, arm, severely; Privates Elijah P. Dowd, arm and body, mortally, since died; Josiah Workman, arm, slightly; Jacob Baker, arm, slightly; Thos. Magourn, arm, slightly; Daniel S. Driden, leg, slightly; James H. Wooddell, leg, slightly; Darius R. Swails, face, severely; Johnson Van Buskirk, mouth, slightly; Joseph McMahon, arm, slightly; William Trott, arm, slightly; Thomas Jarnell, shoulder and arm, slightly.
Missing—none.

Company F, Killed—none.
Wounded—Sergeant David Robins, hand, severely; Privates John Martin, arm, slightly; L. J. Donaldson, leg, severely; Mathias Elliott, arm, slightly; Gaddis P. Hageman, hand, slightly; Robert Johnson, hand, slightly; George Spraker, leg, slightly; Thomas Wright, leg, slightly; A. B. Curtis, leg, slightly.
Missing—none.

Company G, Killed—none.
Wounded—Privates John W. Baxter, head, mortally, since died; Robert Larimore, arm, slightly; A. J. Brake, shoulder, severely; James Grimes, shoulder, slightly.
Missing—none.

Company H, Killed—Privates Urias C. Fulk; Henry Lanmore. Wounded—Sergeant E. W. Quickenbush, arm, slightly; Corporals Dorsey W. Huxley, head, severely; Wesley Criz, face and breast, slightly; Privates Lewis Grim, jaw, severely; Colegit J. Bussy, side, slightly; Russell Lee, arm, slightly.
Missing—none.

Company I, Killed—Corporal C. Miracle.
Wounded—Privates Enoch Fuller, arm severely; Fred. Crow, leg, slightly.
Missing—none.

Company K. Killed—none.
Wounded—Captain Abraham Kaga, acting Major, two field officers being on detached service, shoulder, severely; 1s Ser't, William H. Nogle, throat, severely; Corporal Andrew Wilson, hip, slightly; Privates Oliver P. Bogast, leg, slightly; Henry Clansind, mouth, severely; Regimental Orderly James A. Knox, hip and abdomen, mortally, since died.

List of casualties in the 20th Regiment, O. V. I., at Raymond, Miss., May 12th, 1863:

RECAPITULATION.

RANK.	Killed.	Mortally Wounded.	Severely Wounded.	Slightly Wounded.	Missing.
Commissioned Officers	0	0	2	0	0
Non-Commis'd Officers....	2	2	4	6	0
Privates	8	4	7	31	0
Total	10	6	13	37	0

Five of the six reported wounded have since died.
I am, General, very respectfully, your most obedient servant,
M. F. FORCE,
Col. Com. 20th Ohio.

HEADQUARTERS 20th REGIMENT, O. VOL. INFANTRY,
SNYDER'S BLUFF, MISS., June 3d, 1863.
Brig. Gen'rl CHARLES W. HILL, *Adjutant General of O.:*

GENERAL—I have the honor to report the following list of casualties in the 20th Regiment, Ohio Volunteer Infantry, in the action at Champion Hill, Miss., May 16th, 1863:

Company A, Killed—none.
Wounded—2d Lieut. W. W. McCracken, face, severely; Privates Daniel Harris, thigh, severely; James Clinch, leg, slightly; Ma-

7

jor Rigby, shoulder, severely ; Ira B. Allen, arm, slightly ; J. J. Cremer, hand, slightly.

Missing—none.

Company B, Killed—none.

Wounded—Sergeant John Rheinhart, leg, slightly ; Private Silas Young, head, mortally.

Missing—none.

Company C, Killed—2d Lieutenant Presly McCafferty.

Wounded—Corporal John A. Ferrell, shoulder, slightly ; Private John Hasking, shoulder, severely.

Missing—none.

Company D, Killed—none.

Wounded—Captain V. T. Hills, foot, slightly ; Corp'l M. Risher, arm, severely ; Private Virgil Williams, head, slightly.

Missing—none.

Company E, Killed—none.

Wounded—Corporal Thomas Leggett, hand, slightly.

Missing—none.

Company F, Killed—none.

Wounded—Privates Kelly, hand, slightly ; George Wood, arm, slightly ; William Willis, thigh, slightly.

Missing—none.

Company G, Killed—Private John Eller.

Wounded—Privates David Lawson, shoulder, slightly ; Peter Beaty, head, severely ; Uri Miner, hand, slightly.

Missing—none.

Company H, Killed—none.

Wounded—Privates B. B. Hashman, arm, slightly ; J. P. Tussellman, leg, slightly.

Missing—none.

Company I, Killed—none.

Wounded—Private Abisha McGowan, thigh, slightly.

Missing—none.

Company K, Killed—none.

Wounded—Sergeants Samuel McCobe, leg, slightly ; Dickenshut, hand, slightly ; Privates J. W. Smith, hand, severely ; Daniel Manning, arm, slightly ; George Blakely, back, slightly.

Missing—none.

RECAPITULATION.

RANK.	Killed.	Mortally Wounded.	Severely Wounded.	Slightly Wounded.	Missing.
Com'd Officers.................	1	0	1	1	0
Non-Com'd Officers........	0	0	1	5	0
Privates	1	1	5	14	0
Total	2	1	7	20	0

HEADQUARTERS 20th REGIMENT, O. VOL. INFANTRY,
SNYDER'S BLUFF, MISS., June 3d, 1863.

Brig. Gen'l CHARLES W. HILL, *Adjutant General of O.:*

GENERAL—I have the honor to report the following list of casualties in the 20th Regiment, Ohio Volunteer Infantry, since the commencement of the siege of Vicksburg, May 24th, 1863:

Company A. Killed—none.

Wounded—Private Caleb W. Galliher, head, slightly.

Missing—none.

Company D, Killed—none.

Wounded—Corporal David W. Thomas, shoulder and spine, mortally ; Private John Alexander, chest, mortally.

Company F, Wounded—Albert Hines, hand, slightly.

Company K, Killed—none.

Wounded—Private Jesse Babcock, body, mortally.

List of casualties in the 20th Reg't, O. V. I., at Champion Hill, Miss., May 16th, 1863.

RECAPITULATION.

RANK.	Killed.	Mortally Wounded.	Severely Wounded.	Slightly Wounded.	Missing.
Non-Com'd Officers..	1	1	0	0	0
Privates	0	2	0	2	0
Total	0	3	0	2	0

Also, Privates Columbus Johnson, Co. G, and Jackson Willis, Co. K, serving with 6th Michigan Battery, severely wounded.

I am General, very respectfully, your most obedient servant,

M. F. FORCE,

Col. Com. 20th Ohio.

———

CINCINNATI, April 24th, 1876.

CAPT. D. W. WOOD, *Mt. Vernon :*

DEAR SIR—I stayed home from church yesterday, rummaged over my papers, to get some details of names and dates, and corrected the manuscript of my address accordingly ; and also wrote out my response to the toast "the enlisted men," and mailed them.

I regret that the address does not contain more details of the history of the regiment ; but the addresses of Col. Whittlesey and Gen. Leggett, all of them contain additional facts. For some weeks I have been so pressed—at work always till eleven o'clock, sometimes till two o'clock at night, that it has not been practicable for me to get time, or to get up a wakeful, working spirit.

I enclose $5, $2 50 for the photographs to be sent, one of the regiment, and one of the three Colonels—$2 50 to go on account for the pamphlet of proceedings of the meeting. I should like thirty copies of the pamphlet, and will send the price as soon as I know what it will be.

Your proposed publication of the rolls of the regiment is interesting and really important. I shall want several copies. I have Adjutant Wilkin's original pencil report of casualties of Raymond and Champion Hill, showing the character of the wounds received by each person, and my mem. added, showing that the mortally wounded died almost immediately.

In "Ohio in the War," the writer of the 20th shows quite a number of appointments, when the officers were never mustered in, so that there is some confusion in the roster. The rolls ought to show when the officers were mustered in, and I suppose the rolls at Columbus do show it.

Quite a number of the 20th were appointed in other regiments, as both the McElroy's, George Rodgers, Owens, Curran and others. Such facts ought to appear on the rolls.

When I begin on the 20th I don't know when to stop.

Very truly, yours,

M. F. FORCE.

TOASTS.

THE ENLISTED MEN.

Response—ATTENTION, BATTALION! [*Cheers and Laughter.*]

I see by the response that the regiment is here. But it was not easy to discern in this staid array of solid men of business, and substantial farmers, the rolicking, fun-loving, patient, daring soldiers, who used to sleep on the ground in the rain, wade in rags through swamps, and dash into the midst of battle with equal alacrity and cheerfulness.

Nothing in the war impressed me more than the conduct of the enlisted men; my feeling towards them grew into something like veneration. The first striking fact was the transformation of a multitude of citizens into an army of soldiers. The citizens of a republic have part and voice in all public affairs. They elect the officers of state and direct their action. They obey nothing but the laws which they themselves enact. The soldier has no voice in selecting officers, or directing them; his whole duty is summed up in the phrase, obedience to orders. Such a citizen would seem to be intractable material for a soldier. But when the citizens saw that military law is part of the law of the land, that military obedience is a citizen's duty, they spontaneously complied with all that discipline demanded, and rendered a hearty and thorough performance of duty that compulsion could never exact.

When service in the field was begun and the operations of war were undertaken, the next striking fact was the aptitude of the men for every emergency that arose. If it became necessary to construct or to run a railway, to navigate a steamboat, to print, to telegraph, to build a bridge, men were found in the ranks ready for the work. While this might be the case in an army of any nation formed from the body of the people, I think it was especially an American trait to find men equally ready to overcome emergencies that were new to them. When a freshet in the Big Black River in Miss. carried away the bridge, leaving the pickets on the farther side, exposed to capture, there was not a man in my brigade who had ever tried to build a boat, but before sunset they had planned, built and caulked a bateau, and stretching a rope across the river, constructed a swinging ferry that brought the pickets in. When our division had stepped up to the base of the heavy work near the Jackson road at Vicksburg, and were much annoyed at shells tossed over as grenades, wooden mortars were devised, and I was since told that Corporal Friend, of Co. C, of the 20th, originated the idea; which with a small charge of powder lifted shells just over the crest of the works like answering grenades.

When we were swinging around Atlanta one day, skirmishing the while, the line halted along a rising ground. The men began at once with bayonets, tin cups and sticks to throw up a line of works in their front. Staff officers dashed along to stop them till the engineer could trace a line. But the engineer, on examination, found no change or improvement to suggest.

But the striking fact that presented itself all through the war, was the spirit that actuated the men. There was no difference in material between the officers and the men. At the close of the war a majority of the officers serving in the western army, had entered the service as enlisted men. When our regiment was mustered out, a sergeant Weatherby, had become Lieutenant Colonel. I believe there was not an officer in the regiment, except Colonel Wilson, who had not served in it as an enlisted man. When the 31st Ills. was mustered out there was not an officer in it who had not entered it as an enlisted man. The officers and men were all of the same stuff; but the enlisted men, with their scanty pay, their few privileges, their certainty of enduring hardships, their little chance of winning distinction or glory, could have nothing to excite them but patriotism and duty.

Acting in that spirit, nothing could quench their cheerfulness. It was a perpetual pleasure, riding at the head of the regiment, to listen to the jokes, the banter, the pungent thrust, the quick repartee, the ringing laugh that gave brightness and gayety to the march, and found fun in toiling and slipping through the mud and rain long after midnight.

Anything that could have a comic aspect had to encounter a fusilade of fun. One day, on the return from Water Valley, as the brigade lay at a halt by the roadside, a little old man came jogging along on a mule, and almost buried under a huge dilapidated bell crowned beaver hat. As he slowly passed the column, every man turned on the ground and fired off his joke. One of the 30th Ills. cried out, "Old man, come down out of that hat. I know you are there, I see your boots." The day that the Sibley tents were turned in and the shelter tents were issued, the air rang all day long with banter over the diminutive novelties. When at Grand Junction the clothing wore to rags, and the rags dropped off, so that Gen. Leggett, in an official letter, begged if clothing could not be obtained, an issue should be made of indigo, so that the men could stain their bodies blue. The men found more amusement than hardship in recurring so nearly to the state of Adam in Paradise.

Want of food was treated as lightly as want of clothing. When filing back from Northern Mississippi, rations were scanty to the last degree. I asked a soldier who was standing outside of his tent in the rain, why he was doing so ; he answered, "I want to get wet to make my dinner swell and help to fill up." On the march to Monroe, Louisiana, the hard bread issued was so bad, that when I broke a biscuit on a plate, the pieces all moved about, borne by the worms, unusual for their size and variety. Col. Shedd, of the 30th Ills. told me his men complained of the hard bread. I told him we were away from supplies and had no other. He came to me again to say his men said it would not matter, they would eat it all night and think it was sandwiches.

But all this mirth was only the surface waves that danced and sparkled over profound depths of feeling. In November, 1864, a little before we began the march to the sea, when pay was nine months in arrears, winter was coming on, and then indications of some new enterprise of unknown duration, and letters from home told such piteous tales of want and distress, that the soldiers went apart in the woods to read them, where no eyes could see the tears they could not repress. Not one faltered in his resolve to do his whole duty.

In February, 1863, when we lay at Memphis, preparing for the Vicksburg campaign, in that dark period of the war, when the air was full of discouragement, soldiers received letters from home, urging them to desert. They sat in the snow and wrote in reply: "Father, I have always been a dutiful son. Nothing is so sweet as a letter from home; but if you can write only such letters as this, I would rather never hear from home."

One busy day before Vicksburg, I was told that a soldier wanted to see me. I found him lying on the ground, amid the boom and roar of battle. He was a mere lad. A hole in his breast told the story. He could not speak, but gave me a wistful look.

I said we must all meet our end sometime, and he is fortunate who meets it in the discharge of duty. You have done your duty well. It was all he wanted. His face lighted up with a smile, and he was stiff in death.

This boy fairly represented the enlisted men. The feeling of duty and self-sacrifice filled their souls. They taught me how noble human nature can be. Their uniform came to be the symbol of unselfish patriotism. And even now I cannot see that uniform without a rush of memories, and a thrill of the old emotion.

GENERAL JAS. B. McPHERSON.

RESPONSE BY COLONEL WHITTLESEY.

Although this is a festive occasion, we must not forget the dead.

Through all our joyous greetings there must run a tinge of sadness for those who are not here.

It was by no power of our own that we are now living, while they fell, and were hastily placed in rude graves on the field of battle.

Every one of us should feel it to be a duty to bear all of them in remembrance ; and at these re-unions to bring written notices of the life and character of our brother soldiers, who were not so fortunate as ourselves, but who did as much for the cause as we did. Never let their memory perish.

I presume the memory of General McPherson was referred to me on the supposition, that coming

8

from the shore of Lake Erie, we were personally acquainted. I had never met him, however, until the attack on Fort Donelson; afterward, during the second day at Shiloh Church, he brought me orders from General Grant, while we were on our way to the mouth of Snake Creek, and I never saw him again.

My personal acquaintance with him, is therefore very limited, embracing only a few minutes of conversation, wholly official. Although our troops had met with a great disaster, of which he was a witness, I found him calm, courteous and perfectly clear in giving his instructions.

He rode a good horse, and hurried back along the Owl Creek Road, full of life and vigor, to find General Wallace.

General McPherson graduated at the United States Military Academy, at the head of the class of 1853. He was promoted, of course, into the engineers corps. Until 1861 he performed the usual service of a lieutenant of engineers at Boston, New York, Delaware Bay, and San Francisco, constructing permanent fortifications.

In August, 1861, he was promoted to be Captain of Engineers. In November, Gen. Halleck made him an aid, with the rank of Lieutenant Colonel. From February to May, 1862, he was Chief Engineer to General Grant.

In May, 1862, he was promoted to be Brigadier of Volunteers, and placed in charge of the western railways.

In the attack on Iuka, he commanded a brigade, where he developed so much ability as a general, that he was soon after commissioned Major General of Volunteers.

General Grant not only gave him his confidence as an officer, but formed with him the closest personal friendship. The 17th Army Corps was soon placed in McPherson's hands. We hear of him successfully at Holly Springs, Memphis, Vicksburg, Grand Gulf, Raymond, Jackson, Champion Hill, and again at Vicksburg, all the while growing in the confidence of his superiors.

He was not one of those commanders of whom his inferiors stood in awe. His manners were genial and courteous. He was already a thorough student of the art of war, becoming more and more accomplished in his profession by practice in the field.

In October, 1863, he was entrusted with an army corps, which in Europe is the command of a Lieutenant General.

When the movement to Atlanta was planned, McPherson was given the right wing, composed of the 15th, 16th and 17th Corps, constituting a full army. He had already acquired the confidence of both Grant and Sherman.

The plan of the first movement of the Atlanta campaign involved the capture of the railway in Johnson's rear, at or near Resaca. This was assigned to McPherson. Sherman wished to give Johnson a staggering blow at the outset. His plan of attack was one that appears to be as certain of success as anything can be in war. While Thomas made an assault upon Mill Creek Gap, Schofield with the left wing, came down from the north upon Dalton.

McPherson was ordered south, along the west side of the mountains to Snake Creek Gap, about

half a day's march west from Resaca. He did not
capture Resaca, or hold the railway, and Johnson
escaped. He discovered his mistake before night,
and before any criticism had reached him. His
frank assumption of whatever blame attached to
the result and all its consequences, was in full ac-
cord with his noble character. Sherman was cha-
grined, but even his impetuous nature attributed
the failure only to an error of judgment in regard
to the strength of Resaca.

As this was the only censure which fell upon
McPherson in ten engagements where he held an
important command, should we allow this single
instance to throw a shadow upon his fame?

How many of our Generals have succeeded in
nine battles out of ten?

In the fortunes of war, to win more victories
than he suffers defeats, ensures the reputation of
a commander.

Let us look a moment at the situation of Resaca.
McPherson was not peremptorily ordered to attack
the place, but only to cut the railroad.

The day was well advanced before he could re-
connoitre the works. He perceived that Johnson
had constructed roads from Dalton to Snake Creek
Gap, which was in our rear, and where the trains
were left. In McPherson's judgment, before Resaca could be carried, the rebel army might attack
his trains at the Gap. Although their retreat to
the Gap proved to be an error, I do not see how,
with the hasty information he was able to get, his
conclusions were not sound.

A dare-devil commander would have taken the
risk, and would have succeeded. A calm, intelli-
gent General would have declined it.

Good Generals are not made of dare-devils, but of men who act upon their conclusions, based upon the circumstances.

You all know how he retained Sherman's confidence, and went on winning more reputation, at Kingston, Dallas, and Kenesaw, until the fatal 22d of July, before Atlanta. He was then only thirty-five years of age.

I can say nothing of him more touching or more true, than the brief eulogies of General Sherman and General Grant.

On the fall of General McPherson, Sherman reported the event to headquarters at Washington, as a part of his account of the action, in which he said : "He fell booted and spurred as the gallant knight and gentleman should wish. Not his, the loss, but the country. This army will mourn his death, and cherish his memory, as that of one, who comparatively young, had risen by his merit and ability, to the command of one of the best armies which the nation has called into existence to vindicate its honor and integrity. History tells of few who so blended the grace and gentleness of the friend with the dignity, grace and courage of the soldier."

General Grant was still more grieved by his death, and says of him : " He was one of the most able of engineers, and the most skillful of generals. The nation grieves at the loss of one so dear to the nation's cause. Every officer and soldier who served under him, felt the highest reverence for his patriotism, his zeal, his almost unequaled ability, his amiability, and all those manly virtues which can adorn a commander."

THE OFFICERS OF THE 20th OHIO REGIMENT, AND THE 17th ARMY CORPS.

Ladies, Comrades, and Friends:

Language will not permit me to express my love for the officers of the dear old 20th Ohio Regiment. My time will not permit me to speak of all the living or the dead. It is right and proper for us to meet on occasions of this character, and recount the trials and struggles through which we have passed to preserve this glorious Union, and by these reunions rekindle in our hearts that feeling of patriotism that will always prompt us to respond fearlessly to our country's call, when our liberties are in danger or our political rights invaded.

While I look upon these officers present, my memory is crowded with many dreadful battle scenes, where we left so many of our brave comrades. Joy and sorrow sweep my brain in turn; joyful when I think of the many kindred spirits that are with us on this occasion; sorrowful when I think of the many brave boys whose bones now bleach on southern soil, and whose noble and heroic spirits have winged their everlasting flight to the bosom of the God who gave them.

The Southern Confederacy exists only as the remembrance of a troubled dream; its proud armies have been destroyed; its opulent cities laid waste, and its country made desolate, as the natural reward of its treason.

In these reunions we should only rejoice that we were triumphant in preserving our liberties and the Union, and securing to all mankind within our national border, civil and political liberty, and not rejoice because we have subdued our own brothers ; and while we rejoice, extend that charity and sympathy due a fallen foe, from a conquering and a victorious people.

We have with us to-night, General Force, who bears the lifelong scar of our dreadful struggle while leading us on to victory. Who can forget that dreadful day on the 22d of July, 1864, when the blue and the gray fought hand to hand in dreadful fits of desperation. When Force, Walker and Fry of the 20th fell, wounded upon the field of battle. No, we can never forget them, but will always respect and love them.

Who could forget McPherson, who gave up his noble life on that terrible day, when men who thought it cowardly to shed a tear, wept like a mother, at the loss of her first born babe, when they heard of his death.

We have with us to-night, another officer of the 17th Army Corps, General M. D. Leggett, who fought so heroically in that desperate contest, and led us faithfully and carefully to victory. No, we will never forget them, but when I think of their heroic conduct, I feel proud of them. I love them, and I will let them dwell reverently in my memory through time and in eternity.

In conclusion, let me say, a nobler, a braver set of men never marched beneath the graceful folds of the American Flag, than the officers of the 20th Ohio Regiment, and the 17th Army Corps, and they shall always have my sympathy, my respect, and my love, as comrades in war and in peace.

CHAPLAIN PEPPER'S RESPONSE TO THE TOAST,

"OUR DEAD COMRADES."

Our dead comrades! How solemnly suggestive the toast! In the honored graves in which they sleep to-night, they need not the cold words of mortal tongues to pronounce their praise. They are, this evening, far above the eulogies of the living crowd. Sceptered immortals, enthrowned above the nation's constellation, as was said of the heroes of Salamus. We too may justly say of our noble dead, they went in the blaze of battle from the camp to the stars.

Since that fatal April morning, rich with roses, when the first flash of traitorous guns sent the blasphemous challenge to the stars and stripes, thousands of heroic men have laid down their lives with joy, and implored the stroke of death, for the unity and perpetuity of that land which the sword of Washington evoked, the philosophy of Jefferson approved, and the great arguments of Webster rendered more solid and enduring.

It is said when the illustrious French soldier, Latour d'Aubergne, the first grenadier of France, as he was simply yet honorably called, fell in the service of his country, his name was still retained on the muster roll of his regiment, and when called out by the commanding officer on service days, the oldest soldier would step out of the ranks, and amid the solemn silence of his comrades, reply in these touching words: *"Dead on the Field of Honor."* And so when the muster roll of our American dead shall be called out to future generations,

the Angel of Liberty will point to their sepulchres
and respond: "*Dead on the Field of Honor.*"

Rich triumphs have they won for us and for our
children.   The victories of the war, were under
God, the victories of *the enlisted men.*   I therefore
speak of them first.   I would not take one laurel
from the crowns which adorn the brows of the
mighty captains who led our hosts to victory.

From the patient Grant, from the chivalrous
Rosecrans, from the intrepid Sheridan, from the
brilliant Sherman, from the dashing Hancock, from
that great host of Generals who gathered around
the banner of "Beauty and Glory," as Napoleon's
Marshals around the Imperial Eagle ; but never-
theless our success is largely due to the rank and
file.   Their graves for ages to come will be sacred
spots, where valor shall gain fresh life, and freedom trim her torch.

>They struggled, fell, their life blood stained
>   The cruel Southerner's hand ;
>They clasped their country's flag
>   And cried, God and our native land.
>Let angels spread their wings above,
>   Let flowers forever bloom,
>Let bays, green bays spring forth,
>   To mark the martyr's sacred tomb.

Wherever Columbia plants her standard, the
brave deeds of our dead comrades shall be men-
tioned with gratitude, honor and devotion.

The patriot materlogy is filled up with great and
splendid names.   Their memories rise to my lips
like the sound of the church which I heard in my
infancy.

Shall I speak of Ellsworth, the first to give up
his life for the Union ? of Kearney, the one-armed
hero ? of the eloquent Baker, who went from a

9

Senator's seat to a soldier's grave ? of McPherson, than whom a more stainless knight never drew a sword ? of Thomas, the great hearted ? of Vance, our own Vance, who was torn to pieces by the bullets which he so splendidly defied ? of Andrews, from old Kenyon near by, whom the soldiers loved while living, and wept when dead ?

The necrological list is long, sad and magnificent. The humblest of our dead brothers wears a crown, which like the laurels of Tiberius, shall be forever green, defiant of the lightning and imperishable.

If the winds of heaven could bear our words to the skies, the spirits of the dead conquerers of our liberties would be glad to know that their names and deeds are pious, glorious and immortal. Dead comrades, ye died not in vain ! Rest in beautiful peace ! We swear on your graves, by our hopes of immortality, that the Republic of Washington and Lincoln shall be coeval with the coming grandeur of the son of God !

Movement against Forts Henry and Donelson.

A spirited discussion has been going on during the past year on the origin of the campaign up the Tennessee River, in February, 1862.

This route into the enemy's country had so many palpable advantages, that it probably occurred to many officers long before it was undertaken. Forts Henry and Donelson were the nearest forts on the military frontier, except Columbus.

Between the two rivers an army could march with its flanks covered, and its supplies moved principally by water. Bowling Green was better fortified; had a larger garrison, and was less accessible.

Doubtless, every military man who reflected upon the situation, came to similar conclusions. The reasons in favor of this line of advance were so numerous and easily understood, that their discovery cannot be regarded as an evidence of military genius.

The significance of the present discussion arises from the standing of the various claimants, more than from the importance of the question itself, being now resolved into an inquiry of priority of dates.

Swinton (Division Battles of the War, page 62,) avers that it was suggested incidentally, by Buell and Grant, early in January, 1862.

General Boynton has thrown much light upon the issue, by liberal quotations from the official correspondence. On the 20th of January, General Halleck writes (page 12) to headquarters, "that a much more feasible plan, would be to move up the Cumberland and Tennessee, making Nashville the objective point." For this movement he required sixty thousand men. He had on the Ohio fifteen thousand; had ordered seven regiments (say five thousand) from Missouri, and by the middle of February could send fifteen thousand more, making about thirty-five thousand. If thirty thousand or forty thousand more could be provided, the column could safely move, and adds: "Perhaps the main column should move from Smithland, between the two rivers, by way of Dover, (Fort Donelson) perhaps east of the Cumberland, perhaps west of the Tennessee."

General Boynton states (page 13) from the records, that in *November*, 1861, General Buell urged General McClelland, then in command of the armies of the United States, to permit an advance on Nashville, turning Bowling Green on the right or west, the supplies to go up the Cumberland.

General Grant is reported as having been engaged in preparations for the movement, in December, 1861, without suggestions from McClelland, Buell or Halleck.

The President was then becoming annoyed at the inactivity of the armies. On the 31st of December he telegraphed to Halleck: "Are you and Buell in concert?" Halleck replies on New Year's day, 1862: "Never a word from Buell—not ready to co-operate." On the same day, Mr. Lincoln telegraphs to Buell the same question: "Are you and Halleck in concert?" and receives in reply the same answer as from St. Louis: "No arrangement with Halleck." The two department commanders then began to get acquainted with each other. On New Year's day, General Buell asks of General Halleck: "Is any concerted action arranged for us? If not, can it be? should be done speedily." Halleck replies: "No instructions to co-operate; barely troops to threaten Columbus; hope to be able to co-operate in a few weeks; now impossible.

On the 3d, Buell urges an attack on the center by gunboats, and twenty thousand men.

On the 6th, General Grant wished to discuss the forward movement with General Halleck, which was declined. On the 7th, Buell enquires of Halleck: "Can you fix a day for action in concert?" A reply is received on the 9th, in which are the following phrases: "Madness to operate on Columbus! I know nothing of the plan of the campaign."

General Grant went in person to St. Louis on the 23d, where his proposition was received so coolly that he thought he had given offense. About this time the President's patience became exhausted, and the first executive order was issued, January 27th, commanding all the armies to move on the evening, at latest, by the 22d of February.

It was probably about this time, that the present head of the army held an interview with General Halleck at St. Louis, where it is intimated the plan of the advance up the Cumberland was originated. At page 219, vol. I, of General Sherman's Memoirs, will be found the following statement:

"About mid-winter, 1861-2, *Cullum, Halleck* and *myself* were in a room at the Planter's House, St. Louis, discussing the situation.

"Halleck requested his staff officer (Cullum) to draw on a map before them, the position of the rebel line, and asked: 'Where is the proper line to break it?' Either Cullum or I said: 'Naturally, the center.' Halleck drew a perpendicular line near the middle of their front, which coincided with the Tennessee River, and said: 'That is the true line of operations.' This occurred more than a month before Gen. Grant began his movement, and as he was subject to General Halleck's orders, I have always given him (Halleck) full credit."

Thus far it does not appear that the plan had been thought of at Washington. General Buell had considered a movement east of the Cumberland in November. General Grant had begun preparations for it in December, hoping to get the consent of General Halleck.

Some days before the President's order, General Grant and his scheme was decidedly discountenanced at headquarters. The executive order, however, encouraged him to go on with his preparations. It had also the effect to stimulate General Halleck, who sanctioned his plan early in February.

Having thus briefly gone over the premises, I introduce an official copy of a letter written by myself to General Halleck, in November, 1861, on the subject of this movement. It originated in this way: General Halleck was expected at Cincinnati on the 18th of November, on his way to assume command of the department of Missouri.

I was on General O. M. Mitchell's staff as Chief Engineer of the department of Ohio, and had a conversation with him upon the line of advance, substantially as it is stated in the letter. General Mitchell, on my suggestion, intended to bring the subject to General Halleck's attention that evening, but he came so late, and left so early in the morning that it was not brought up. He suggested that there would be no impropriety in a letter from me to General Halleck, whom he thought would receive it kindly. Governor Morton, of Indiana, was at our headquarters on the 19th, and the subject was again discussed, for it appeared the route by way of those rivers had occurred to him.

Under these circumstances the letter of the 20th of November was written, and its receipt acknowledged from St. Louis on the 22d.

LETTER TO GENERAL HALLECK.

"CINCINNATI, OHIO, Nov. 20th, 1861.

"Major General HALLECK, *St. Louis:*

"SIR—Will you allow me to suggest the consideration of a great movement by land and water, up the Cumberland and Tennessee Rivers:

"1st. Would it not allow of water transportation half-way to Nashville?

"2d. Would it not necessitate the evacuation of Columbus, by threatening their railway communications?

"3d. Would it not necessitate the retreat of General Buckner, by threatening his railway lines?

"4th. Is it not the most feasible route into Tennessee?

"Yours, respectfully,

"CHAS. WHITTLESEY,

"*Col. Chief Engineer, Department of Ohio.*

"War Department, Adj't General's Office, Dec. 11th, 1875.

"Official Copy,

"L. H. PELOUSE,

"*Ass't Adj't General.*"

On this I do not propose to offer many comments.

In General Halleck's letter of January 20th, he refers to a movement following the valley of those rivers, evidently not then considered in detail.

My letter of two months previous may not have influenced him, but his expressed views are the same.

At that time, General Buell had not corresponded with him on the subject. General Grant had already given his reasons in favor of the movement, which General Halleck considered entirely premature. It is perfectly clear, however, that it did not *originate* among the group of officers at the Planter's Hotel, *about mid-winter.*

Whatever military merit there was in its conception in January, 1862, cannot be lessened by a conception, the same in substance matured in November, 1861, and then on file in the office.

www.ingramcontent.com/pod-product-compliance
Lightning Source LLC
Chambersburg PA
CBHW021626270326
41931CB00008B/895